# What Color Is Your Money?

## YOUR PERSONALIZED ROAD MAP TO FINANCIAL SUCCESS

# TOPE GANIYAH FAJINGBESI
CPA, ACA, MBA

D1710963

FIRST EDITION

Editing by Indie Author Counsel.
Cover & interior design by Indie Author Services.

ISBN: 978-0-9890868-0-6

Published by House of Ganiyah LLC.

# CONTENTS

# INTRODUCTION

Dear Reader,

Congratulations on following your passion by embarking on the journey toward entrepreneurship, along with over 1 million people in the U.S. every year.

Even if you are still debating whether or not to "get into the game" or even if you think entrepreneurship isn't your thing, this book will help you learn how to manage the business of "You." Seeing yourself as a critical business that must not fail should be one of your biggest missions in life.

In the decade and a half that I have been an accountant, I have met and worked with various types of organizations and individuals. However, my biggest passion remains helping small business owners. I have compiled the most essential advice and insights into this book in the hope of reaching those struggling with financial management issues. I believe that by implementing the simple tips presented here, you can make sure your business venture and the business of "You" grow sustainably in today's tough business environment.

I deliberately begin this book by focusing on you and your personal finance style (the color of your money), before delving into business management tips because only a financially healthy individual can manage and grow a profitable business. I purposely developed the book by identifying fifteen of the most important questions business owners have asked, or should have asked, in my fifteen years as an accountant. Next, I answer those questions, offering you fifteen keys to business success.

I thank you for allowing me to have this conversation with you. I know the time and resources you are investing by reading this book will make a big difference in your journey towards financial success, which is what I wish for you.

Sincerely,
*Tope Ganiyah Fajingbesi*
CPA, ACA, MBA

# CHAPTER 1

## WHAT IS MY MONEY COLOR?

*"Understand how your relationship with money determines your level of financial success."*

Money Color is a simple and non-scientific system that I developed to help individuals understand and improve their relationship with money. Your Money Color is essentially your money personality expressed in easy-to-understand terms. From my experience dealing with clients over the years, I have essentially classified people into five categories represented by the colors—Green, Blue, Yellow, Grey and Red.

Green folks are the growth machines of every economy; a green person thinks every dollar should be invested.

Blues like to save every dollar. They are very careful with investments because they hate to lose money; they won't take big risks.

Then there are the Yellows, who see money as a tool for happiness. They are not necessarily in debt but, when they see something they want, they buy it regardless of whether it is in their budget or not. They believe that since they work hard, they should reward themselves with the finer things in life.

Next are the Grey folks, those who, for either religious or other beliefs are very conservative with regards to money. They don't even like to think about money. They just want enough of it to take care of their basic needs. Even though these people are the hardest ones to talk to about investing, they are really the best and most patient investors especially in socially responsible enterprises because they are willing to wait for long periods to earn returns on their investments.

The final color is Red, a person who is perpetually incurring debts, even for the flimsiest wants. They don't pay close attention to financial management and haven't yet taken the time to understand issues surrounding their personal finance. Well, now is the time! I hope the Reds reading this book will contact me so that we can work together to resolve the issues they face with financial management.

Every color category has strong points and weak points. The strong point of the Green, a group of passionate and motivated people, is that they are always creating wealth. They are employers of labor. Every economy needs them to grow. But the problem with Green is that they can get too carried away with investing, make poor choices and rack up a lot of debt for ventures that won't succeed. For instance, my Green friend who visited my village of Ijebu, waterside in the southwest region of Nigeria, during a particularly hot time of the year noticed that none of the 100,000 households had air conditioners. So he saw a perfect business opportunity to import and sell air conditioners from the United States to everyone there. He thought he could easily make a net profit of $100 on each unit. Not having the cash to invest in this business, my friend quickly put a "good" business plan together, obtained a loan from the bank and loaded a shipping container with the first 10,000 units. Sounds like a good plan, right? Wrong. None of the units have been sold since they arrived six months ago. That is because Mr. Green left out some key details – the potential buyers do not have a stable and sufficient supply of electricity to power the units. My kinsmen are mostly farmers and fishermen who spend most of their time outdoors and, most important of all, Nigeria's electricity system is incompatible with that of the United States, so he has to spend a significant amount of money to alter these air conditioners before he can sell them. These details not only shrunk his market size but also turned a $100 profit per unit into a loss-making venture.

Blues are fiscally responsible, they know how to save and live within their means. However, the problem with Blue folks is their failure to understand that they won't get rich by simply keeping their money under their pillows. They need to be encouraged to invest and step out of their comfort zone a bit, as long as it's done with a little bit of care. The real issue with Blues when it comes to investing is really the feeling of helplessness and loss of control associated with investing their hard-earned money in businesses managed by others. But there are creative ways to resolve this issue. Instead of investing all your funds in the stock market and then spending sleepless nights and endless daytime hours monitoring the stock activities beyond your control, why not join forces with like-minded partners to start a small business that deals in something you

## NOTES

# CHAPTER 2

## WHERE SHOULD I START?

*"Financial health begins at home."*

Do you live from paycheck to paycheck?

Do you supplement your paycheck with credit cards, payroll advances or other types of loans?

Are your finances strained because of unemployment?

Do you find it hard to balance your checkbook?

Do you simply get overwhelmed with the issues of money and finance, and rather not deal with them at all?

Don't beat yourself up if one or more of these apply to you. Dealing with financial matters can be quite stressful. However, the fact that you are reading this book shows that you wish to make your financial situation better. So, let's get to work!

Money issues cause unbelievable conflicts and stress in individuals and families. Many of us don't know how to deal with this "elephant in the room." However, the best way to begin is by forming the habit of taking stock of your financial health on a regular basis, because financial health checkups are just as important as periodic medical checkups. We need to lose financial baggage just like we need to lose excess body fat, and the way to do this is by striving to make healthy choices with money just as we do with food. In short, we need to work hard at living our best financial life, even if it takes effort and is not something that falls into our laps.

So how do you begin the critical migration towards living your best financial life? My first suggestion is for you take a pen and a piece of paper and draw what I like to call the "DOES" project. Divide your paper into four columns (an example follows this section) and document the following:

Your Debt: List how much and to whom you owe money for your car, house, and credit cards. Include tuition, medical bills and all other items you have acquired on credit, and have yet to fully pay off. Even if you pay your bills when due, you still need to know how much you owe in order to get a complete financial picture of your situation.

What do you Own? In this section, list the value of the items you own, that is, the amount you could sell them for today. Include bank account balances and any investments and property you could sell if you needed to. Include expensive jewelry and your cars if they are fully paid for. Do not include items of little or no resale value, such as clothes, shoes and home decorations that may be difficult to sell. You should also exclude items you acquired on credit and listed under Debts that you have not yet fully paid off. The total of this section will tell you how much cash you could come up with (if the need arose), today.

Now compare the value of what you owe to what you own. If the value of what you own is higher than what you owe, great! You will need to continue making good choices. If the reverse is the case then, like dieting, you need to work harder to cut some of the excess fat and pay closer attention to your lifestyle.

One way to do this is to differentiate your wants from needs, and ensure that you put a lot of thought into financial obligations before assuming them. If you make choices based on other people's perceptions or expectations, you will continue to land in financial trouble. The people you are struggling to impress will not come to your rescue when disaster strikes, which is inevitable if you keep up an unsupportable lifestyle.

**Table 2.1: An example of the first part of the DOES project**

| Your Debt | Amount Owed | What You Own | Value |
|---|---|---|---|
| Home Mortgage | $165,000 | House – Current Market Value | $120,000 |
| Car Loan | $10,000 | Car – Current Market Value | $5,000 |
| Credit Cards | $4,000 | Savings Account Balance | $2,000 |

| Your Debt | Amount Owed | What You Own | Value |
|---|---|---|---|
| Salary Advance | $6,000 | Stocks (Investments) | $3,000 |
| Other Bank Loans | $3,000 | | |
| Student Loans | $12,000 | | |
| Total value of debts | $200,000 | Total value of items owned | $130,000 |

Verdict is poor. You owe more than you own, so you need to lose some weight!

I recall advising a young student several years ago against obtaining additional student loans to finance a new car and vacation trips, but he wouldn't listen at the time. All my attempts to make him see that he was foolishly "eating his dinner in the morning" fell on deaf ears. I explained to him that there would be time in the future to enjoy those things, but he did not heed my advice. I was therefore not really shocked a couple of years later to hear him complain about his level of debt and how servicing those debts was hindering him from enjoying his income.

Now let us move on to the other half of the DOES plan: (Again, an example follows).

- How much do you Earn? Now that you have established how much you owe and own, the next crucial step is to determine how much you earn from all sources every month. You should exclude one-time gifts and non-recurring income, but include employment and other constant income here. This amount represents the maximum amount of money you can and should spend each month.

- How much do you Spend? This is the most important part of this entire exercise. How much you spend and what you spend it on can determine whether you sink or swim financially. The key to financial success is "cutting your coat according to the size of your fabric," which means you should only buy items you can afford.

illusion or might not happen until they are at the end of their working life. Or, even when they do save, they eat up their savings without thinking too much about it. The truth is that if you cannot save when you earn $100, you probably won't be able to when you earn $100,000. So, even if you must start small, start early and just do it!

### Maintain Self-Discipline.

Your biggest barrier to maintaining healthy cash reserves for a rainy day is your own self. Your ability to prioritize, delay self-gratification and, most importantly, separate your wants from your needs can make or break you financially. So, be sure to think about expenses carefully before making them, otherwise you will continually struggle to pay your bills with nothing extra to save and no hope of achieving your financial goals. Expenses that need to be funded from cash in your savings account require extra and more careful consideration on your part.

### Budget Your Savings.

You should try to maintain a personal budget no matter how much or how little you earn, and savings must be a prominent line item on that budget, just like your other expenses, such as rent, car and food. The first and most important person that should be paid every month should be you. After all, you are the one who works for the income, and the best way to pay yourself first is to save.

### Avoid Debt.

How can you maintain your savings when you owe far more than you own? Keeping money in your savings accounts when creditors keep knocking on your door is almost impossible. Although there are unfortunate life events that cause some good people to be in huge debt, many of us land in trouble because of our inability to maintain self-discipline. So remember to cut your coat according to the size of your fabric.

ESTABLISH SAVING CONTROLS.

All of us have the ability to stray far from our goals, therefore, it is important to establish strong saving controls. Saving controls are those conditions that force you to save. Examples include: establishment of payroll direct deposit into a savings account, maintaining a savings account in a separate bank from the one you frequent, and keeping your savings account debit card and other account access documents at home instead of in your wallet so you don't have ready access to them during a moment of weakness. These were the controls I implemented after my savings blunder in 2003, and I am happy to say I was able to get back on track and save enough money to buy my house in March 2005.

## NOTES

# CHAPTER 4

## WHY DID THEIR VENTURES FAIL?

*"Avoid failure by laying a foundation of
strong financial management."*

This chapter talks about that man on your street that keeps launching a new business every two years. Yes, the same one that launches a "powerful" venture after a year of mourning the crash of the last big idea he made so much noise about. I am talking about that serial entrepreneur who can't seem to lock down that one good venture that will finally launch him into the millionaire's club. Is he just jinxed or are the ideas just wrong? I don't think so. Let us look at the case of Joe – a man I have known for several years and watched launch several "big" business ideas, ranging from a bakery to commercial transportation and even trading in power generators and residential real estate, all within a period of 10 years. Sadly none of these businesses succeeded. In the case of the bakery, he failed because he had no marketing plans in an already saturated market and his lenders were not patient enough to allow him ride out the rough times.

Okay, so you don't have that neighbor, but surely you have clicked on that cool business website and strangely got an error message saying they are no longer around, yet you see Google history and stories from the big showcase they put up just a few months ago. So why did their business just die? Did they suddenly go broke? Well, going broke might be one of the problems, but they just didn't wake up broke. Here are some of the problems that may have nailed their coffin and how you can avoid them.

UNDERSTAND YOUR TIMING.

The issue of timing is best explained with the case of Titi, who saw a fantastic opportunity to generate rental income by building a block of apartments close to the site where a new university campus was being built. She invested her life savings in the project, but that was not sufficient. She still needed to raise about 20% of the project cost. So, she began applying for bank loans. After hitting nothing but road blocks with the bank, she decided to seek out private investors instead, and she succeeded. She promised the lender that she would repay the loan within two years. Although the university campus was ready when the loan was due to be repaid, Titi's apartments were yet to generate enough revenue to enable her to repay the loan because the first set of students were not yet admitted. She eventually had to sell some of her ownership in the building to a new investor to repay the lender when she could no longer withstand the pressure. Had Titi considered the university's timing when she was discussing repayment terms with the lender, she could have negotiated a longer repayment period or sought other lenders. In fact had Titi read this book at the time of planning the project, she would have sought a "Grey" investor, who would be more inclined to granting her a longer repayment period.

## GET SERIOUS ABOUT YOUR MONEY.

There are so many business owners with smart business ideas, whose faces light up when they talk about their products, services and dreams, but whose businesses crash simply because they didn't pay enough attention to the financial management aspects. Financial management includes documenting your visions and expectations for your business, maintaining and understanding financial statements, and implementing solid internal controls.

Recall our friend Joe, the serial entrepreneur who started several businesses but couldn't keep any of them solvent? Joe could tell how many loaves of bread the bakery produced within an hour but he couldn't tell how much it cost to produce one loaf of bread. He could tell what size and type of bread you were holding in your hand with his eyes shut just by smelling it, but he couldn't tell how many loaves of bread the bakery had to produce and sell in a month to reach a break even point. (A break even point is the point at which the business makes neither a loss nor a gain. This is the minimum income level the business owner strives to attain, as amounts below this point result in losses.)

## SPEAK THE LANGUAGE.

One of the reasons Titi, our friend who built some apartments near a campus under construction, was unsuccessful in getting a bank to lend her money was because of a language barrier between her and the banking officers. She approached the banks with the most beautiful idea, an idea she was sure would generate enough income for her to comfortably repay the loan. However, she did not take the time to build good budgets and reasonable financial projections, the language that serious investors understand. So, frustrated was she by all the rejection that she chose to take a loan with unrealistic repayment terms. Therefore, whether you are looking for initial investors to start your business or to expand an existing business, it is important to communicate your vision and expectation of the business in clear terms in the form of budgets and financial projections. This foresight and preparation will show prospective lenders that you have given careful thought to your proposal and that you strongly believe in the success of the idea you want them to invest in.

## Understand Your Money Color.

Joe's color is Green, so he invested in any and every business idea that seemed to make business sense without carefully understanding what each venture really entailed. All he saw in each of his proposed ventures was an opportunity to make money, but he made the mistake of not seeking the opinion and assistance of experts before investing in an enterprise like selling power generators. It is not only folks in the Green color category that can run into these sorts of problems. Mr. Red, who hasn't invested the time and discipline required to fix his money behavior, will end up using business funds to settle personal debts. Ms. Grey, who invests in a venture that does not match her value system, will not devote the time needed to guide the business to success. Mr. Blue will crash his business if he refuses to re-invest business profits in projects that will ensure growth and sustainability. And Ms. Yellow will find herself bankrupt if her investment decisions are solely based on her tastes and desires for luxury.

## Understand the Business Environment.

Make sure you do your homework before you sink your entire life savings into that "big" business idea. Have answers to some hard questions like, what makes you qualified to run that particular business? Don't invest in a restaurant just because your mother, who doesn't like to hurt your feelings, keeps telling you that you are the best chef she knows. You have seen those contestants on the talent shows, the ones who come with their entire clan, but sound so horrible when they open their mouths to sing. We all wonder why they didn't get feedback from a couple of strangers before auditioning, instead of relying on the rave reviews of their tone-deaf relatives that they are the next big thing after Michael Jackson. Well, some entrepreneurs have this problem too. In addition to building technical expertise, it is also important to understand all aspects of the business environment, such as relevant government regulations, customer preferences, vendors and competitors, prior to launching your business. What are your key weaknesses that may prevent you from succeeding and how do you plan to address them? Being an entrepreneur means you have to make tough decisions and hold difficult conversations, otherwise you may land in trouble.

## NOTES

# CHAPTER 5

## WHAT IS THE DIFFERENCE BETWEEN CASH AND PROFIT?

*"Profit is what remains from your income after all expenses are paid."*

We focused on your individual financial wellness in the previous chapters. Now we move on to discussing how you, the business owner, can successfully steer the business in the right direction. One area where many, many business owners encounter difficulty is financial management. You work so hard to put out a good product or service and make money, but it seems like you are struggling to put water in a basket with many holes. You simply don't know where that money goes at the end of the month or year. This problem is so common that it almost seems like part of the territory. But it isn't, and it doesn't have to be.

Many business owners ask, "What is the difference between the money I have in the bank at the end of the month or year, and my profit? Are they the same?" It's so easy to see the money that is left in your bank account as profit, but that is not necessarily the case. Your cash flow is the difference between the money that comes into your business and what you spend to finance business operations, additional investment in the business (by you or outsiders, such as lenders) and other activities such as buying assets for the business. Profit is the difference between sales revenue, also known as business income and the costs of doing business during a specific period. It is possible for a business to make profits yet have no cash in the bank. This can happen if goods or services are sold on credit and customers are much slower in paying, while the business is quick in paying its own vendors. A small business owner needs to pay closer attention to cash flow than profits.

Not recognizing the difference between cash and profit is one of the biggest mistakes a small business owner can make. Small business owners need to prepare a monthly cash budget in order to make sure they know their cash flow positions.

Now let us explain this difference with a non-business scenario. Assume that you decide to host a party for the oldest of your 3 children, so you invite 20 of his friends over, however, you take your youngest child to the babysitter on the day of the party, so there are 22 children in your garden - 20 of your child's friends and 2 of your own children. If somebody asks you how many children are in your garden, you will say 22. That number of children, just like the cash balance in your bank account does not fully belong to you. On the other hand, if the question was how many children you have, you'll say 3. That number like your profit is correct even though only two of your kids are present at the party.

When making plans to spend the cash you have in your bank account, you should first of all calculate and set aside the portion that does not belong to you. For instance, you should calculate the amount that belongs to customers who have made deposits in advance for products or services that you have not yet delivered, and the amount you need to pay suppliers who have sold goods or services to you but whom you have not yet paid. A big balance in your bank account may be misleading, because it can be easy to think it's all yours. Always think about your cash balance like the children in your garden, some will have to go back home when the party is over.

Your profit, on the other hand, is actually your gain from the business, some of which may not be included in your cash balance because customers still owe you. Profit is the difference between the value of what you have sold and what it cost you to buy/make the sale and run your business.

As a second example, let us assume that you are in the business of selling pencils and that you ordered $800 worth of pencils from your supplier but have only paid him $300 with a promise to pay the remaining balance ($500) at the end of the year. Let us also assume, for the sake of keeping this example simple, that you do not have any other business expenses apart from the cost of the pencils. During the year, you sold all of those pencils for a total of $1200, and all of your customers have paid you. Your bank account has a balance of $900 at the end of the year but your profit is only $400 (the difference between your sales of $1,200 and the cost of the pencils of $800). Your bank account, however, shows a much larger balance because $500 of that balance belongs to your suppliers.

**Figure 5.1: Analysis of your Profit from the Sale of Pencils**

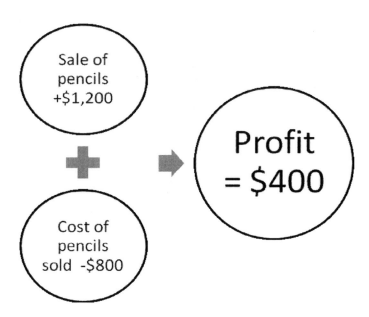

Ultimately, knowing the difference between your cash balance and your business profit will help you avoid the common mistake of thinking that all the money you see in your bank account is your profit and therefore available to be spent.

This fundamental understanding takes us to the next common mistake that I see business owners making, using their business money to pay for personal expenses.

## NOTES

# CHAPTER 6

## HOW CAN I AVOID COMMON CASH MANAGEMENT MISTAKES?

*"Keep business and personal finance separate, for starters!"*

One of the biggest mistakes that business owners make is spending business cash on personal expenses. This rather destructive practice is especially common among small business owners who keep business checkbooks, debit or credit cards in their purses or wallets, right next to their personal cards. Say you need to buy something for the house and you realize that you don't have personal funds to pay for it, but you know the business account has some money. So, you can use that since it is your business, right? Wrong, you can't do that.

If you really want your business to grow, you have to consciously step aside and allow it to blossom. There will come a time when you will be able to draw some money from your business, but you need to plan and time this carefully in order to ensure that you don't kill the business before it even has an opportunity to prosper. Your business is like a plant: when you plant a seed in the ground, you have to wait for the tree to grow before plucking the fruit or flowers, right?

There are many ways to "step aside to let your business blossom." Most of the work has to come from you - from your mind and from focusing on your desire to grow your business. You need to be disciplined, especially during the first three to five years. Things might be tough for you personally, but you need to keep that focus. Erecting barriers, such as using completely different banks for your business and your personal life, may also help you. What do I mean by different banks? I don't mean just having different bank accounts. I mean if your business account is with Sunshine Bank, you should keep your personal funds with Moonlight Bank so that when you go into Moonlight Bank, you are not thinking, "Oh, my bank account is so depressing, let me just take some money from the business." It really helps to keep both entities, that is, you and the business, completely separate.

Another thing to avoid is paying business bills with cash. This is particularly tough for businesses that have cash sales. However, it is important to form a habit of depositing your entire cash sales into the bank account promptly and settling expenses through checks or electronic transfers to empower you to effectively separate yourself from your business. Keeping your business cash "lying around" is as tempting and dangerous as keeping cans of soft drinks in the refrigerator when you are diabetic. It is really important to try as hard as you can to keep your business transactions separate from your personal transactions (even if you run your business from your basement) in order to achieve success.

It is also important to carefully plan and compare your practice regarding cash payment (to vendors), to your policy for receiving cash from your customers, assuming you buy and sell items on credit. You should collect cash from your customers much quicker than you pay your vendors, otherwise you may find yourself cash strapped and constantly piling up additional debts to run the business and settle your vendor accounts.

I hope you will take away the following tips from this chapter:

- Quit robbing from Peter to pay Paul. Avoid co-mingling of personal and business funds by maintaining separate bank accounts in physically separate banks.

- Create an accounting trail by depositing 100% of business funds into the bank and pay all business bills with checks, without exception.

- Keep good financial records. This is the best way to know if some or all the parts of your business are doing well or not.

- Always hope for the best but prepare for the worst. Your personal assets may be at stake if there is a law suit and the courts see that business funds were frequently used as personal funds.

## NOTES

# CHAPTER 7

## WHY DO I NEED A BUDGET?

*"A good budget can transform your business practices."*

Predicting future business income and expenses can be really difficult for most business owners. However, this should not stop you from doing your best to prepare budgets. I often hear business owners complain about the efforts they put into business planning at the beginning of the year, only to get half way through the year and find that what is actually happening with the business is very different from the initial plan. If you have experienced this, you may wonder if it is really worthwhile to create a budget. And if you do create a budget, what are you supposed to do with it? You prepared a budget in January, now it's June, and things just haven't turned out the way you hoped. What are you doing wrong?

These are questions that I get asked a lot by many business owners. There are several issues here, so let me explain them one by one. First, let us assume you get on a plane, and as you begin to settle down and buckle your seat belt, the pilot begins to make the following announcement:

*Welcome to flight number—*
*Oops, I am drawing a blank;*
*I cannot remember what the flight number is.*
*We are happy you chose to fly with us to—*
*Oh my God, I cannot remember where we're going.*
*I am not sure what altitude we will be flying at today.*
*We will just see what the weather looks like when we hit the skies.*
*Our flight time will hopefully be between—*
*Ha, let me think—*
*Hmmm, between 2 and 5 hours.*
*Why don't you just sit back, relax and enjoy the flight.*

I bet if that aircraft door was still open, you would be running out of the plane leaving your bags behind! Okay, now stay with me for a second; see that horrible picture in your mind you have of this clueless pilot. That poor image or negative impression is exactly how your business looks to a potential investor when you tell him/her that you have no budget.

Your budget is written documentation of your desired destination and how you hope to get there. If instead, the pilot had said:

*Welcome to flight number DU 123 to Lagos.*
*Our cruising altitude will be 34,000 feet.*
*We are anticipating some rough weather around Akure.*
*So we will climb to 37,000 at that point.*
*Our flight time today is 2 hours and 8 minutes.*
*Please sit back, relax and enjoy the flight.*

You will feel confident that the pilot is experienced and has done his homework. So, you feel at ease and that you are in good hands. That feeling of ease and comfort is what a potential investor feels when they see that you have a good budget.

Last year, one of my client firms was able to successfully negotiate a loan from its parent company more than 6 months before the cash was needed, simply because the business maintained a budget and had anticipated the significant cash outflow it would require for business expansion. There was absolutely no embarrassing situation of unpaid vendors or business shut down because the managers had anticipated the increase in cash outflow. Unfortunately, I also worked with a client, whose business was acquired due to many problems, including financial struggles during the last year. Upon reviewing the operations reports, I realized that had the managers paid attention to the declining business numbers, maintained a budget that incorporated cost reduction strategies, that most of the headaches would have been avoided.

Also, even if you are not looking for investors, a budget is still essential to successful planning of your business. It helps to keep you in check and to remind you of the goals you have set for the business. Some of my clients express shock when I say that having a budget at the beginning of the year is a key ingredient for making profits. Why do I say this, they ask? A budget pushes you to identify your costs, which are the primary drivers of the price you charge customers for your products or services. Your budget will also show you and other relevant stakeholders (such as investors) expected total sales, cost of goods sold, operating expenses, profit and taxes, all of which will play key roles in your business management, especially marketing plans.

Now that you know why you need to have a budget, what happens if during the year you find yourself going off course? The best way to handle this is to look at a budget as being fluid and dynamic, not static. A budget should not be a once-a-year financial plan of all revenues and expenses, prepared and then left to gather dust all through the year. A savvy business owner will compare their budget to actual activities on at least a monthly basis. For example, if you planned to spend $300 on electricity for your business in the month of January, but your bill comes to $600 at the end of the month, you need to step back and think about what is going on. Can you plan better, for instance? Can you control this cost better, for example, by shutting off the air conditioners or heaters in the parts of the building you are not using, or run the big machines during the off-peak electrical rate times? Or is your budgeted amount simply too low and not reasonable?

**Figure 7.1: Budget vs. Actual Comparison During the Year**

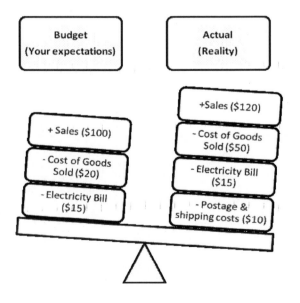

Your budget for future months can be adjusted during the year, especially if you have new information that renders your previous estimates useless. A good ingredient for keeping good and beneficial budgets is to keep yourself accountable as your business moves along, that is, to periodically compare, weekly or daily if necessary, actual activities and results to your budget.

So now that you know that you need a budget and have to review it to correct for differences between budgeted versus actual revenue and expenses, what items and how much of these items should be included in the budget? If you are a first-time business owner, you will not have the benefit of prior experience, but you can look at businesses that are similar to yours to see what expenses they are incurring. The Internet, libraries, small business development centers and small business groups are good sources that help you conduct this research.

On the other hand, experienced business owners should review prior years' expenses to get ideas of what items and amounts they should budget for this year. Experience, they say, is the best teacher.

*See the Do-It-Yourself section for a step-by-step process showing how to build a monthly budget. The example I use there is for a bakery; however, the steps are the same regardless of what your business is.*

## NOTES

# CHAPTER 8

## HOW CAN I FACE FINANCIAL STATEMENTS WITH CONFIDENCE?

*"Let me explain two important statements you need to understand."*

Over the years I have had lots of business owners tell me that financial statements intimidate them. They don't really know what these statements mean, how to prepare them, or which ones to prepare. In response, I have developed an analogy to explain the most essential aspects of financial statements so that anyone can tackle them with confidence. This chapter will also tell you the two financial statements you need to better understand your business.

Financial statements are really like pictures. So, why do we take pictures? We take pictures for memories. And we women take pictures to see what looks good on our faces and our bodies. We also use pictures to determine what areas we need to work on, right? For example, I might look at my picture and say, "Oh my God, I didn't think that my eyes were this puffy. I need to do something." That's what a picture shows you. It's a snapshot of what you look like. And that's exactly what a financial statement is. Never mind all the complicated things you hear out there. A financial statement is just a picture of your business. It shows you exactly what your business looks like at a specific point in time.

There are two key financial statements that I always encourage small business owners to get familiar with – the income statement, also called the profit and loss account, and the balance sheet, both of which will be discussed in this chapter. But first, let us go over some important background information that is critical to financial management success.

### Choosing the Right Financial Systems for your Business.

It may come as a surprise to some readers, but 9 out of 10 small business owners I have met don't have defined systems to monitor their financial transactions. I have seen all kinds of systems ranging from business owners who pile up invoices and receipts in shoe box to those who tell me that they keep records in their heads. Let us go back to the picture example in the previous chapter: Keeping your financial records in a shoebox is like trying to look a certain way, buying the clothes that you think will fit without keeping mirrors at home and without taking any pictures of yourself. How would you know if you are achieving the right look or not? There are many ways to keep good financial reports regardless of your size. In order to ensure that you don't spend time you could be using to manage the business operations, sweating over financial statement preparation, I advise you to hire a book keeper. If you are unable to afford one, particularly if your business is really small, you can keep financial records yourself using simple software such as QuickBooks™ and Quicken™.

I know the subject of Financial Management may sound really complicated to some business owners. Perhaps, it sounds like something that should be left to the financial experts to sort out, but it is really something that every business owner must deal with in order to achieve financial success.  Sure you may need help, but even if you make enough money to hire an expert, you still have to know the right questions to ask. I have noticed that the faces of a lot of entrepreneurs light up when I ask them about their products or services, but they don't have the answers to questions like, "How much does this product really cost? Or, "How much does it cost you to deliver your service? Or "How much is your profit?" But not knowing these facts is a recipe for disaster. Many businesses with great ideas fail within the first three to five years because owners are busy thinking about their great ideas without paying close attention to the numbers. How much does it really cost to produce your products or service? How much should you really sell your product for to ensure that you can stay in business and even expand? How much profit or loss did you make last year/ month/quarter? What is working and what needs to be changed?

These are questions you can answer when you pay close attention to the financial management aspect of your business. So what is financial management? It simply means understanding the monetary implications of business activities and using this understanding to make good decisions, and planning, and controlling business activities to achieve success. One of the basic elements is maintaining good financial records. Your financial reporting method should be chosen based on the size of your business, skills level and ease of access. Financial management should not be a painful and inefficient process that keeps you from focusing on your business. For example, if you are a small business owner with no access to a computer and very few transactions, you could keep your records in a ledger. You may use one page to record everything that you sell, the next page for everything bought from vendors, and the next page for everybody that owes you money. That is the beginning of keeping a financial statement.

It is truly that simple. At the end of the day, somebody might help you put it all together and tell you what that day's picture of your company looks like. Or if you have access to a computer and/or have a lot of transactions, you may use simple programs such as Microsoft Excel, or any of the readily available small business accounting software.

The real challenge for many business owners is to understand what the financial statements really mean and which numbers to focus on. This is why we will discuss the income statement and balance sheet in this chapter.

## INCOME STATEMENT

This is the statement that shows you what your income and your expenses are during a specific period (for example, a year), so that you can see how much gain or loss you made from your activities during that particular period.

The three main parts of the income statement are:

### Sales (Revenue or Income)

This is the amount received (or due to be received) from customers in exchange for your services and products. This includes cash already received from customers and amounts owed to you by customers who are yet to pay for goods/services already purchased. The tricky part of this amount is that it excludes the cash you have received from customers who are yet to receive goods or services paid for. For instance, if you are in the business of manufacturing school bags, and customers paid you in December of the current year for school bags that will not be delivered till the following April, the amount you received from those customers cannot be considered income until you deliver the bags to the customers. The most important thing to consider when calculating your sales amount is whether you have provided the goods or services. If you have, then you have earned that money and can count it as part of your income for the period.

**Cost of Goods Sold**

These are cost items directly related to the manufacture or acquisition of the product or service you are selling. For instance, if you are in the bag manufacturing business, your cost of goods sold will include the cost of buying the leather or other material used to manufacture the bags, and wages paid to the laborers who sewed the bags together, but it will exclude the salaries paid to the driver of your delivery truck and your receptionist because these are not directly related to the manufacturing process.

Examples of cost of goods sold for a business owner selling mobile phone recharge cards will include the cost of buying the cards/air time from the telecommunications company. The most important point to note is that your cost of goods sold should only include those items without which the product or service you are selling will not exist.

The difference between your sales (income/revenue) and your cost of goods sold is your Gross Profit or Loss.

**Operating Expenses**

These are the costs associated with running your business entity. Going back to the bag manufacturer example discussed above, the salaries of the delivery truck driver and the receptionist will fall into this category, as well as the shop rent paid by the recharge card retailer. The difference between the gross profit and operating expenses is the Net

Income or Loss.

You should note that the expenses listed in the sample income statement above do not include the owner's personal expenses because the business income statement records the activities for the business and not the affairs of the owner. Withdrawals made by the business owner are recorded in the balance sheet, which is also discussed in this chapter.

**Figure 8.1: The Income Statement**

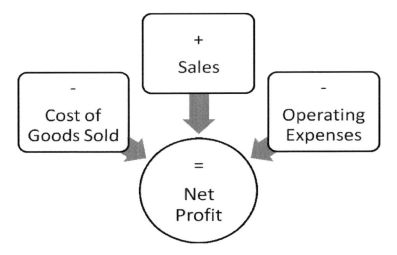

Let me use a familiar nonfinancial topic to explain this concept. Let us assume that you are trying to lose weight, so you step on the scale and decide that you want to lose a couple of pounds. You start exercising and counting calories when you eat. Tomorrow, when you look at your food diary, you'll see you consumed 1,800 calories and burned 500 calories while exercising. The net amount of calories your body consumed for this specific day is 1,300 calories, right? If you understand this example, then you can understand what the income statement is. It is a statement that shows the income your business generated and the costs your business incurred during a specific period. It shows what you have sold and what it cost you to make or buy what you sold. That is, what it cost you to run your business.

**Figure 8.2: A Sample Income Statement**

OFC Sample Company

Income Statement for the Year Ended December 31, 2012

| | |
|---|---|
| Sales | $1,000 |
| Cost of Goods Sold | ($200) |
| **Gross Profit** | **$800** |
| Office Rent | ($150) |
| Office Supplies | ($50) |
| Office Electric Bill | ($50) |
| Staff Salaries | ($50) |
| **Net Profit** | **$500** |

## BALANCE SHEET

Let's go back to the weight loss analogy again. The balance sheet is the result that you get when you step on that scale. If you step on the scale and it says you weigh 220 pounds, that's your balance sheet. That is the financial statement that shows you what your business is worth today. Just as your weight is affected by the calories you consumed and burned during your exercise, the value of your business is also affected by the results of your business activities (income and expenses over time). The balance sheet answers the question, "What is my business worth?" It shows what your business owns (assets), owes to others (liabilities) and how much your stake is in the business as at a particular date (owner's equity). If you have been withdrawing money from your business (and documenting it) without carefully timing and planning this, your balance sheet may indicate that you are actually no longer the owner of the business. It is now owned by your creditors (the banks and other people your business owes).

The major categories of the balance sheet are:

## Current Assets

These are items owned by your business for a short period, usually less than one year. Inventory (stock held for resale), cash in the bank, and the amount owed by customers, fall into this category. These items can be easily converted to cash.

## Fixed Assets

These are items owned by your business that have a life span of longer than 12 months. Buildings, machines and production equipment fall into this category.

## Current Liabilities

These are amounts due to others within one year. For instance, the amount owed to vendors, suppliers and employees.

## Long-Term Liabilities

These include amounts owed to other individuals or corporations, which are not due within one year. Let us assume you started your child care business on January 1, 2013 with a loan of $15,000 from your father, which you don't have to repay until December 31, 2016. This loan of $15,000 is a long-term liability unless it were due to repaid before January 1, 2014. In that case, it would be classified as a current liability because it is due within one year.

## Owner's Equity

This is the owner's real stake in the business. It is the sum of initial capital invested and profits accumulated over the years that have been re-invested into the business (Retained Earnings), less withdrawals made by business owner for personal (non-business) purposes (Drawings). Note that the use of business funds by the owner in this example to pay for non-business expenses reduces the owner's overall stake in the business. Let us assume that you invested your savings of $5,000 into your new business of selling shoes on January 1 2012, then during the year you withdrew a total amount of $800 to buy groceries for your house and also to pay for your son's after school care. In addition, you also took one pair of shoes worth $100 for your own use without paying the business. These are bad business practices Mr. or Ms. Yellow may be guilty of. Your owner's equity, which is the amount you own in the business is now $4,100 ($5,000 - $800 - $100). Notice that your ownership is now smaller than the $5,000 you originally invested in the business.

**Figure 8.3: The Balance Sheet**

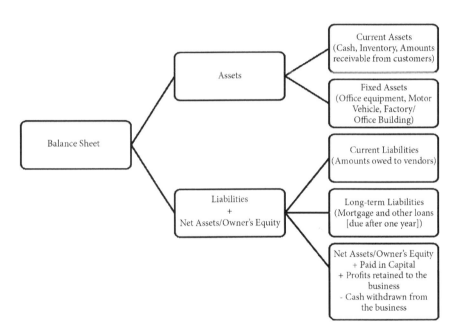

**Figure 8.4: A Sample Balance Sheet**

OFC Sample Company
Balance Sheet as of December 31, 2012

ASSETS:

| | |
|---|---|
| Current Assets | $1,000 |
| Fixed Assets | $2,000 |
| **Total Assets** | **$3,000** |

LIABILITIES:

| | |
|---|---|
| Current Liabilities | $100 |
| Long-Term Liabilities | $1,100 |
| **Total Liabilities** | **$1,200** |

NET ASSETS/OWNER'S EQUITY:

| | |
|---|---|
| Initial Capital | $2,000 |
| Retained Earnings | $500 |
| Drawings | ($700) |
| **Net Assets/Owner's Equity** | **$1,800** |
| Total Liabilities & Net Assets | $3,000 |

The balance sheet gets its name from the following simple equation:

Total Assets = Total Liabilities + Net Assets/Owner's Equity

In the case of OFC Sample Company, you can see that the total assets of $3,000 equals the sum of total liabilities of $1,200 and net assets of $1,800.

## NOTES

# CHAPTER 9

## WHICH OF THESE NUMBERS SHOULD I REALLY KEEP MY EYE ON?

*"These are three key financial numbers to focus on."*

While there are many good numbers that you should know in order to keep up with the health of your business, at the very least, I believe that each business owner must determine and understand the three numbers I will explain in this chapter.

## Net Profit

What is your net profit at the end of the month, quarter or year? That number is your sales less all of your costs for that period. Assuming your sales figure (which you can easily obtain from your income statement) is $1000, and all of your costs, which include the materials you bought for production, your rent, staff salaries, marketing costs, and taxes for that period, add up to $800. This means that you made a gain of $200. In this example, $200 is a 20% net profit margin ($200 divided by $1000). Why should you determine this figure? You need to because it is the amount that is available for you to either take out of the business, since you are the owner, or to reinvest back into your business to grow it.

This is an area that gets a lot of business owners in trouble. They go ahead and withdraw money from the business for personal purposes without first calculating this number to determine if the business actually made a profit and what amount that profit is. Let us assume that after calculating all the costs for the period, you realize that it adds up to $1,200, and not $800 as mentioned above. This means that the business made a loss that period, and there is really no profit for you, the owner, to take a share of.

Making a loss is not the end of the world, it is an indication that you should take a look at your business model and make changes. Perhaps you need to cut costs? Increase prices? Increase sales volume by attracting more customers? If you do not calculate, understand, plan and hold yourself accountable to your net profit margin, then you may be slowly killing your business.

## Net Assets (Owner's Equity)

This is the true value of your ownership in your business. A small business owner that I was working with recently said to me, "Someone asked me the other day how much of my business I own and I had no idea what he was talking about. I thought I owned 100% of my business!"

Again, maintaining good financial statements should make determining this number easy, because the answer is right there in your balance sheet. Your net assets figure is the difference between what your business owns (land, buildings, equipment, inventory held for resale, amounts receivable from customers), and what it owes (bank loans, mortgage for business property, taxes owed and amount owed to vendors). It is like your weight, the number you get when you step on the scale. Weighing yourself is an important part of the weight loss journey (because a number which you are unhappy with is the best motivation for you to change your eating and exercise habits). A net assets number that is continually declining from year to year or the unfortunate situation where your calculation shows a net liability (your business owes more than it owns), signals trouble and calls for changes.

Another mistake that small business owners frequently make, which I have discussed in previous chapters is frequently "stealing" from themselves. What I mean by stealing from yourself is that you pay your personal bills from your business just because you see cash sitting there when, in actual fact, this practice is reducing your ownership in the business and greatly limiting your ability to meet your obligations to vendors and grow the business.

## Cash

The popular saying cash is king is actually very true in the business world. Even if your business is making big profits and your net assets look really good, if you are cash strapped, you will have problems and may go bankrupt. Vendors, investors, and even customers will most likely measure your liquidity by your cash balance and they will feel more comfortable doing business with you if your cash balance looks healthy. Your business needs cash to pay salaries, pay monthly bills and vendors. You need cash to make investments that will grow your business, such as machinery and technology. In addition, your ability to respond and adjust to unexpected situations is limited if you are cash strapped.

So how can you ensure that that your cash balance is healthy, especially if you sell to customers on credit? As noted in Chapter 6, one good tip is to ensure that you collect amounts due from your customers earlier than you pay your vendors. For instance, if your credit terms for customers are that they pay within 30 days, you may want to negotiate 45-day payment terms with your own vendors. A situation where you agree to sell to customers on credit but pay cash to your vendors may leave you in a desperate scramble for cash all the time.

Also, ensure that you plan accordingly, as emphasized in the budgeting and planning chapter. Building and maintaining a budget forces you to know your business and plan your cash flow accordingly. For example, tying your cash down in inventory that won't sell for the next 6 to 9 months is poor planning. Instead, buying goods for resale close to the point in which there is high demand for them, helps manage your cash flow. However, such intricate planning is only possible if you take time to understand your business and build good budgets.

## NOTES

# CHAPTER 10

## HOW MUCH INVENTORY SHOULD I KEEP?

*"Keep financial statements and understand your numbers."*

If you are like some business owners I know, you may find yourself at the end of the year still carrying the same products from the beginning of the year, or even from the previous year. So many business owners want me to tell them how much inventory is too much and how to maintain enough so that their customers do not experience annoying backorders.

Again, it goes back to maintaining financial statements and understanding your numbers. If you have been in business for more than two years, you can begin to see a trend, but only if you keep financial statements. For instance, last year's sales may be very helpful in predicting future sales. You may notice a trend, but that trend can only become apparent to you if you have taken pictures of your business regularly by maintaining financial statements. Not having done so means you will not be able to accurately predict either sales or inventory levels, which in effect greatly lessens your chances of financial success.

You might even know in your head that "a lot" of customers come to your store during the month of August, but what is "a lot?" In business, you cannot rely on vague ideas to make key decisions, such as how much inventory you should carry. Instead, financial decisions should mostly be primarily based on historical data and sound planning. Let's assume you are in the business of selling school supplies, and the last two years in August you sold $50,000 worth of school-bags, but you didn't sell school bags during any other month in those years. Then you know that you don't have to buy schoolbags this January or even in September, but that you should buy school bags in June or July so that you can sell them in August. And when you buy the bags, you should buy about the same volume you sold during the past two cycles. This is a simple example but a powerful reason of why you have to keep financial statements and take the time to understand the trend(s) of your business. Plus, in addition to watching your own business, you must keep a close eye on the business of your competitors as well.

## How is the Competition Doing?

It is important to keep a close eye on the competition, because their activities can affect every aspect of your business, from sales volume and product pricing to inventory carried and marketing expenses. Your competitors' financial statements may not be publicly available if they are small and privately owned businesses. Nevertheless, there are still many avenues for keeping an eye on them – you may take surveys of customers that have done business with them or use the internet to check for useful information about them. I recall reading that Sam Walton, the founder of Wal-Mart, used to go into Kmart's stores to look at layouts and other things when he was just starting his own business.

Maybe you sold $50,000 worth of school bags last year during "back to school" and the same two years ago, but you now have a competitor whose store is right next to yours. That person may be planning to take some of your business, but your understanding of your numbers and your business environment can save you from headache, strengthen and even increase your share of the market. For example, you can use sales records to identify the major customers for the past two years, and reach out to them in June and July and say, "Instead of you coming to the store next month, why don't you order online or over the telephone and let me deliver the bags to you?" Or you may offer discounts if they place orders in advance or offer free gifts if they buy multiple items from your store. These are examples of things that can help protect and even expand your market share.

## Managing Slow-Moving Inventory

What happens to the remaining five hundred children's bags from last season, the ones with a cartoon character that is no longer popular? Should you wait until this year's school season to try and sell them? Or should you try selling them off at half price now, so that you can make room for this season's hot new items? In addition to managing inventory levels, many business owners incur significant losses on

slow-moving or obsolete items in stock. One of my clients had dif-
ficulties selling a particular brand of T-shirts and shopping bags, yet
instead of feeling sad and sorry for herself, she branded these and
turned them into promotional items, which she then gave as incen-
tives to customers. The end result was that the otherwise slow-moving
items then turned into marketing expenses, which helped to increase
sales of other items in the store.

Now that you are aware that keeping close tabs on inventory is imper-
ative for the financial success of your business, you will not encounter this problem next year because you will review and understand
the trend in your sales numbers prior to ordering your next batch of
school bags. However, let me share some tips that will help you resolve
this situation if you are struggling with it.

As long as the sale of your slow-moving product doesn't pose a dan-
ger to the buyer (for instance, expired food or drugs), and there is no
indication that holding on to the items will result in significant future
gains, such as potential for an increase in selling price, you should sell
off the items to free up cash for your business. This is where careful
promotion and deals to customers come in. You can creatively pair a
hot new item with a slow-moving item to get customers to notice the
older item and increase your sales. You may also offer discounts, but
you should exercise caution here and remember the recurring advice
in this book – understand the numbers. Unless there is absolutely no
alternative, you should not sell the items at a price which is lower than
the cost of purchasing it. It is really important to understand the cost
of purchasing or manufacturing each one of your products beyond the
purchase price. We will talk more about cost and pricing in the next
chapter.

## NOTES

# CHAPTER 11

## IS THE PRICE RIGHT?

*"Set your price for profit."*

The price you charge your customers directly affects your cash flow and profits, two things every business owner is naturally concerned about. If there is one question that I wish every business owner would ask themselves every time they set a price, it is, "What factors should I consider?"

There are five things that I believe every business owner must consider when setting prices. The first thing is the true cost of manufacturing, or acquiring the product you are selling. If you are manufacturing your product, this will include the cost of raw materials, the labor of the people who are going to put it together, and other costs directly associated with manufacturing the item.

If you are not manufacturing, but buying to resell, then what is the cost of buying the items from the manufacturer or wholesaler? For instance, if you are selling cars, you need to determine the cost of buying the cars and getting them to your warehouse, showroom or lot. Obviously, it is critical that your price should not be below this cost. Let us say, for example, you are selling pencils and you buy the pencil from the manufacturer for $1.50. If you then turn around and sell this to your customers for $1.10, you have shot yourself in the foot.

The second factor that should be considered is the cost of operating your business, which could include your business' rent, utilities, marketing and advertising expenses and staff salaries.

The third thing that you need to determine is your desired profit (as a percentage of sales, this is known as profit margin). Most business owners are in business to make profits and there is nothing wrong with having an amount that you wish to gain on each item you sell. After all, this is one of the key numbers that will keep you in business. It is okay if you set your price high and later have to reduce it a bit but you should still start by knowing your desired profit margin.

The fourth item to consider is the price your competitors are charging. You may determine that the cost of manufacturing your items, combined with business operating expenses and desired profit amount, make your product or service significantly more expensive than that of your competitors. In this case, you will either have to find a way to cut costs and/or reduce your desired profit, otherwise you may lose customers to your competitors.

This brings me to the final pricing "tool" that every business owner should know. You will need to identify what makes your business different. What do you have that your competitors don't have? What are those products exclusive to your business, and valued by the customer, that can earn you bigger profits because your competitors don't have them?

Let us say you are selling children's toys and, after coming up with all your cost analyses, the Dora the Explorer cup should be priced at $3. However, your competitor down the street sells it for $2.50. Why would I as a customer buy this cup from you at $3 when I can buy it down the street for $2.50? But you know what could happen? The remaining 50 cents you are losing on the Dora cup sale can be absorbed by the Dora umbrella that all children like, but which no other retailer in the area is selling. The bottom line is that to be successful in any business, from soup to nuts, you must understand your products, costs, your competition, customers, and your desired profit and, most importantly, what differentiates you from the rest of the pack.

Now that you know the key financial statements that you should maintain, how to maintain them, how their information can help the growth of your business and how to understand costs and price your products and services, it is time to learn how to attract investors particularly when you wish to expand the business with new capital.

## NOTES

# CHAPTER 12

## WHY DO POTENTIAL INVESTORS KEEP RUNNING AWAY?

*"Make your business a money magnet with strong financial statements."*

So, you are at a point in your business where you have really got some momentum going. You are starting to attract customers, demand for your products or services is increasing and now you need an infusion of cash to grow the business to meet that demand. But you find it difficult to get banks or anyone else to lend you the money you need. With so many positive things going for your business, you may wonder why the lenders aren't lining up at your door.

Why is it that some small businesses are able to get bank loans while others really struggle? The key is to make the potential investor feel safe that the money invested will not be lost. Here, again, is where those financial statements come in.

Picture these scenarios: You are at the bus stop and it is raining, so you desperately need a ride. The first car comes along and the driver pulls up next to you and says, "Hop in." You are shocked that the driver of this tiny car, that already has six passengers in it, wants you to hop in. Hop in to where? The trunk? He must be kidding, right? There's absolutely no space for another passenger in that car. You wave them away.

The next car comes along, the driver stops and offers you a ride, but the car is filthy. You can see a lot of junk in the car, but you are so desperate because it is raining, that you think, "I can manage this." You try to open the door and it falls apart. Really exasperated now as well as soaking wet, you say, "You know what? Just leave me in the rain."

Finally, a third car comes along and it is a beautiful and clean car, plus it has enough room for three passengers. You flag the driver to stop and give you a ride. Finally, a car that looks clean and safe, right?

This is exactly what business owners need to remember when they are approaching potential investors. The impression that you give as the face of your business, as well as how you run your business greatly impacts their faith in you as well as your company. Banks or other investors do not want to invest in your business if you don't look like you believe in that business, or if the business doesn't seem organized or likely to succeed. The best way to prove to a potential investor that you believe in your venture and that it is likely to succeed is to ensure that you have a carefully prepared business plan, which should include a budget and prior years' financial statements (if you have been in business for more than one year). Your business plan should also show growing demand for your product or service and your marketing strategy for turning that demand to sales opportunities for your business.

For example, you can go to a bank or an investor and say you are going to invent an airplane that will take passengers from California to Japan in twenty minutes. And you may talk a good game, but if you don't have the numbers to back it up, you may not succeed. Investors want proof or to be convinced that you can succeed, so that they will get their money back when the time comes.

For starters, they want to see that there is actually a market for your product or service. That proof is your set of financial statements and your budget. When you go to the bank with financial statements that look really horrible, or with no budgets or financial statements, what you are saying to the investor is that you don't believe in your business, but you really think they should. Put yourself in their shoes. What would you think? Crazy, right?

So, to get investors interested in you and your business, you need to be that business manager with a clear vision not only of where you have been (as evidenced by accurate financial records), but of where you want to go (using budgets, forecasting and planning), and how you will get there. The bottom line is this: You wouldn't set foot in a restaurant with nasty looking tables and more flies than patrons. Instead you would opt for the one next door with clean floors, smiling faces that welcome you and food that makes you feel good. So why expect an investor to give you their hard-earned money, with hopes that someday they may get it back, even with a little interest, unless you have the plan to convince them? They want to believe in you, to see it in your eyes, to hear the passion in your voice, to see your business working and to have their financial questions answered with certainty because of well-maintained and accurate financial records.

## NOTES

# CHAPTER 13

## HOW DO I NAVIGATE THE BUSINESS TERRAIN DURING ROUGH TIMES?

*"Check your financial statement for holes that can be plugged."*

In the last chapter, we looked at how to get banks to invest in your company when things are going well. In this chapter, we will be looking at what you need to do when things get rough, those times you feel it might be time to throw in the towel. There may come a time in the life of your business, or perhaps you find yourself there now, when you really wonder whether your business can be saved or if it's a lost cause. Bank loans and financial management aside, you find yourself putting in so much energy, focus, time, passion, and money – indeed, you are putting your self into the business, but it just seems like you can't catch a break. Maybe you can't pay yourself for the long hours you put in, or maybe you don't have enough money to hire people to take the work off your hands. So, instead of the business working for you, you are working for the business and yet you are barely staying afloat.

If this sounds like your situation, you are not alone. But before you give in to what seems inevitable, let us go back to the weight loss example again. You cannot say for sure that your weight loss battle has been completely lost until you have stepped on your scale and taken a picture to check your weight and see how your clothes look on you. This is the same for your business. You cannot say with certainty that a business is a lost cause until you have looked at the numbers.

Starting or closing your business should never be a purely emotional decision. I recently worked with a business owner who was ready to close down her business. She just didn't think it was working and she was quite frustrated. But what I did with her – which is what I advise everyone who is in this situation to do – was to prepare her business' financial statements.

My first answer to her every question and clues to solve her business puzzle lay within the financial statements. They were the picture, the scale, the food diary. So, do like my client did and prepare your financial statements to see exactly what the true picture of your business is. Find where the holes are, and determine whether they can be plugged before giving up.

What this close examination will really show you is whether the business is healthy or not. In this woman's case, after piecing together her financial statements, I realized that she didn't really own the business anymore. She was shocked when I told her this, but I helped her realize that indiscriminately withdrawing money and goods from the business for personal purposes over the years had eroded her ownership in the business. In fact, the business now technically belonged to the banks and other people she owed.

Yet, without preparing financial statements, she had thought her business was a sinking ship. But I showed her it wasn't. She was actually making money and the business had great potential. But without looking at her financial statements, she would not realize that what she really needed was a lifestyle makeover. She needed to separate herself from the business in order to let it grow. She needed to allow the business grow without interference. Her habit of withdrawing cash from the business was killing it slowly and eroding her ownership in the empire she was struggling to build. In addition, she had to implement stronger internal controls to mitigate risks of employee and customer theft. Beyond these measures, I also taught her how to price her products to ensure profitability. I told her that the actual cost of buying the items to resell, other costs of operating the business, her desired profit margin, the uniqueness of the item to be sold (whether an item is exclusive to her store or generally available in the market place) and of course, the prices charged by competitors, all were important factors to consider in pricing her products.

Like the woman in the above example, you simply can't know whether your business is salvageable until you prepare your income statements for the previous three or four years to see the trend. The trend can detect problems including declining sales due to a shrinking market size, or increases in cost of goods sold or various business expenses. You also need to prepare your Balance Sheet to see what your business owns and owes, to best gauge your level of ownership in the business.

Other statements like the Cash flow statement will show the sources and uses of your cash for selected periods.

If you have a shoe store and you started selling some shoes online, instead of selling all the shoes in the store, but are still paying a huge amount for your store rent, your financial statements will show you how much that rent is taking from your profit. Now that you see where money is leaking away, you must take action to stem the tide.

Can you renegotiate some of the loans that you owe so that you can have more time to repay the loans and invest the money you have in the business instead of using it for loan repayments? Maybe you have excess inventory that is never going to move. Why not sell it, even at cost if you have to? Financial statements make your problems stick out like a sore thumb, show you where you are wasting money and what is draining your resources and preventing your business from being as healthy as it can be.

You can look at the picture and say, "You know what? I want to lose some weight around my arm, just as you can say, "I want to cut my overhead costs."

Therefore, my first advice to any business owner who is going through rough times is always to first prepare financial statements for at least three years, if they have been in business for that long. If you haven't, prepare them for as long as you have been in business so that you can see what exactly is happening. Look at what costs you can get rid of or what products you can sell more of.

You might have a business in Raleigh, and another one in Charlotte. They are both in North Carolina, but the one in Raleigh is not really moving. Nobody is really buying anything from you there. So you should ask yourself tough questions like: Why am I wasting my time there? Why am I paying salaries and rent in the shop? Why not just close that Raleigh shop down and move it all to Charlotte, or close both and sell everything online if delivery costs less than rent? These are things that you can really see from your financial statements before you decide to keep going or to quit.

## NOTES

# CHAPTER 14

## WHAT DO INTERNAL CONTROLS MEAN?

*"Internal Controls can Save/Boost/Grow your Business."*

If you are like many business owners I have talked to, you are proba-bly wondering what "internal controls" mean. Every business owner - however large or small your business may be—must design and implement suitable internal controls.

Let me explain internal controls. Would you drive a car without brakes? Even if the car looks new and beautiful, you still want brakes to stop it in case things get out of control, right? Well, that's what inter-nal controls are. They are the brakes of your business. They are those things that help prevent your worst fears, (e.g., employee theft), from coming true. They are the policies that help mitigate the risks that your business is naturally exposed to, because every business has some level of risk associated with running it. There are risks of theft, fraud, obso-lescence of your inventory, or even natural disaster.

Examples of internal controls include simple things like the require-ment that you, as a small business owner, sign all business checks instead of delegating such a sensitive duty to your shop clerk just because he has been working for your family for twenty years. One of my client's rather "trustworthy" Accounts Payable Clerks managed to write and sign three company checks totaling over $15,000 to her hus-band, without being caught. She was able to do this because of a lapse in internal controls. Her job functions included keeping the check-books, writing the checks, signing the checks and reconciling the bank accounts. The fact that she was responsible for all these finance roles created a big opportunity for her to steal from the company when her husband lost his job and they were facing eviction from their home. What did my client do to avert future occurrences? The checkbooks were henceforth kept in a locked safe in the business manager's office, the new accounts payable clerk still wrote the checks, but they had to be signed by the business manager. The bank reconciliation was also performed by a different employee other than the accounts pay-able clerk and the business manager. Segregation of finance duties is a good way to prevent and/or detect fraud. This may be tough when the business has only a few employees handling the finance function, so I recommend that the business owner handle all financial oversight functions in such cases.

Other examples of internal controls include:

- Writing checks to specific vendors rather than to "Cash."

- Writing checks in sequential order to make it easier to detect stolen ones.

- Not issuing blank or pre-signed checks.

- Making daily bank deposits, not only to facilitate bookkeeping, but also to reduce the risk of theft and fraud.

- Keeping checkbooks and financial records in secure locations.

- Restricting and password-protecting access to key online sites such as bank accounts and customer orders.

- Eliminating, reducing or restricting use of business credit cards, especially for personal purposes.

- Monitoring outstanding items on bank reconciliations. To ensure that you don't lose sight of this, set up recurring reminders on your computer or even telephone calendars, put sticky note reminders to perform reconciliation on your desk and notices on your wall.

- Comparing your budget to actual financial statements regularly to help you promptly detect deviation from your plan.

- Requiring, obtaining and filing original invoices/supporting documents for all expenses.

- Segregating financial duties and isolating the chain of command for those employees as the business grows and matures.

- Developing accounting and operations manuals and ensuring that they are followed.

- Limiting theft and obsolescence of inventory by performing both periodic and unscheduled counts.

In summary, internal controls should be designed in such a way that they are compatible with the size and nature of your business, but with a firm understanding that, as the brakes of your business, they are the tools that help your business not only stay afloat, but grow bigger and stronger.

## NOTES

# DON'T FORGET TO...

1.  Keep a budget—it is the road map to your destination.

2.  Maintain good financial statements—they are like pictures that show you what your business looks like.

3.  Understand the numbers—they may seem complicated at first, but you will get the hang of them once you know the goal. You can always seek help from me if needed.

4.  Sign all checks—don't let someone else take the money you are working hard for.

5.  Keep a close eye on inventory—plan, don't build up unnecessarily. If you are selling tangible products and have inventory, make sure you do surprise and unscheduled counts.

6.  Use bank accounts—avoid keeping cash in hand. The risk of theft is high when there is cash lying around.

7.  Deposit all bank sales daily—do not pay bills with cash. Use checks and keep records. Trust me; this will keep you sane when you start wondering what you spent all the money on at the end of the year.

8.  Separate your business from yourself—even if it is being run out of your basement. Don't be an obstacle to your success.

9.  Treat your business like a person with a future—open a savings account, invest carefully, and gradually build reserves for future expansion.

10. Understand the Three C's: Your costs, competitors and customers—they are the key to setting the right prices for your goods and services.

## NOTES

# DO IT YOURSELF

## QUIZ

### Section 1 – True or False?

1. The best time to begin saving is when you land your dream job and are comfortable.

2. The cash balance in my business bank account is the profit available for me to withdraw.

3. The income statement is also known as the profit and loss account.

4. Total assets is a number equal to the sum of total liabilities and net assets (owner's equity).

5. Cash withdrawn from the business bank account for personal use is considered part of business operating expenses and should therefore be captured in the income statement.

### Section 2 – Fill in the Blanks.

Okoro Ventures, a small business which sells salt to local restaurants, has provided the following information about business activities during the year 2012. Please review and help build an income statement and balance sheet for the company.

- Mr. Okoro started his business with $10,000 cash withdrawn from his personal savings account at the beginning of the year.

- He bought office furniture and equipment worth $3,000 for business use.

- He bought 200 bags of salt from his vendor at $15 per bag. The total cost was $3,000, (Okoro Ventures still owes the vendor $1,800 of this amount).

- During the year, the business sold a total of 100 bags of salt for $3,000 ($1,000 of this amount has not been received from customers).

- Other business expenses paid during the year included: Office rent - $600, Electrical bill - $200, Bank charges - $50, Staff salaries - $250, Taxes - $100.

- Mr. Okoro paid his younger sister's school fees of $800 from the business account.

**Okoro Ventures**

**Income Statement**

**For the Year Ended December 31, 2012**

| | | |
|---|---|---|
| Sales | $3,000 | |
| Cost of Goods Sold | ( Fill in ) | Question 6 |
| Gross Profit | ( Fill in ) | Question 7 |
| Office Rent | ($600) | |
| Bank Charges | ($50) | |
| Office Electric Bill | ($200) | |
| Staff Salaries | ($250) | |
| **Net Profit before Taxes** | $400 | |
| Taxes | ($100) | |
| **Net Profit after Taxes** | $300 | |

**Okoro Ventures**

**Balance Sheet As of December 31, 2012**

**ASSETS:**

| | | |
|---|---|---|
| Current Assets: | | |
| Cash | (Fill in) | Question 8 |
| Accounts Receivable | $1,000 | |
| Inventory | (Fill in) | Question 9 |
| Fixed Assets | $3,000 | |
| **Total Assets** | $11,300 | |

**LIABILITIES:**

Current Liabilities:

| | |
|---|---|
| Accounts Payable | <u>($1,800)</u> |
| Total Liabilities | <u>($1,800)</u> |

**NET ASSETS/OWNER'S EQUITY:**

| | | |
|---|---|---|
| Initial Capital | $10,000 | |
| Retained Earnings | $300 | |
| Drawings | <u>(Fill in)</u> | Question 10 |
| **Net Assets/Owner's Equity** | <u>**$9,500**</u> | |
| **Total Liabilities and Owner's Equity** | **$11,300** | |

## Section 3 – Multiple Choice

11. Which of the following should a cake baker include as part of cost of goods sold?

    a. Flour

    b. Office rent

    c. Marketing materials

    d. All the above

12. Examples of savings controls include:

    a. Establishing payroll direct deposit

    b. Keeping savings account withdrawal documents at home

    c. Both a and b

    d. None of the above

13. In order to ensure success, financial goals should be:

    a. Simple

    b. Clear

    c. Measurable

    d. All of the above

14. Which of the following numbers should not be included in the income statement:

    a. Sales on credit
    b. Owner's personal expenses
    c. Office rent expenses
    d. All of the above

15. Which of the following is included in the balance sheet?

    a. Office rent expense
    b. Sales
    c. Salaries
    d. Office furniture and equipment

# ANSWERS

1. False
2. False
3. True
4. True
5. False
6. Cost of goods sold = $1,500

Number of bags sold during the year = 100

    X

Cost per bag (amount paid by Okoro Ventures to its vendor) = $15

7. Gross profit = $1,500

| | |
|---|---|
| Sales | $3,000 (including sales on credit) |
| Less: Cost of goods sold | ($1,500) |

8. Cash = $5,800

| | |
|---|---|
| Mr. Okoro's initial investment | +$10,000 |
| Office equipment and furniture | -$3,000 |
| Cash paid to bags supplier | -$1,200 |
| Cash received from customers | +$2,000 |
| Business Expenses | -$1,200 |
| (Office rent, electric bill, bank charges, salaries) | |
| Drawings | |
| (payment of sister's school fees from business funds) | -$800 |

9. Inventory = $1,500

Number of bags unsold at the end of the year = 100

X

Cost per bag (amount paid by Okoro Ventures to its vendor) = $15

10. Drawings = $800

Use of business funds to pay Mr. Okoro's sister's school fees reduces Mr. Okoro's equity (ownership) in the business.

11. A  12. C  13. D  14. B  15. D

# ADDITIONAL RESOURCES

# BUILD A BUDGET

| Sample Monthly Budget for Sweet Abby Bakery | |
|---|---|
| **Description of Business** | Cake Bakery and Sales |
| **Budget Date** | January 2014 |
| **Period** | 1 Month |

## Step 1 - List all ingredients required to bake cakes

| Item |
|---|
| Flour |
| Sugar |
| Eggs |
| Butter |
| Baking Powder |

## Step 2 - List all office and cake-making equipment

| Item |
|---|
| Oven |
| Cake Mixer |
| Baking Pans |
| Display Shelves |

## Step 3 - List all other bakery and shop expenses

| Item |
|---|
| Sales Clerk Salary |
| Baker's Wages |
| Gas and Electric Bill |
| Shop Rent |
| Advertising |

## Step 4 - Estimate Sales (units)

| 1,000 | A |
|---|---|

## Step 5 - Determine Selling price per cake

| $15 | B |
|---|---|

## Step 6 -Calculate Total Sales Value

| $15,000 | C = A x B |
|---|---|

## Step 7 -Calculate Cost of Ingredients

| Item | D Quantity | E Cost to purchase quantity stated in column D | F Number of cakes quantity in column D can produce | G = E/F Cost of baking 1 cake | H = G X 1,000 Cost of baking 1,000 cakes |
|---|---|---|---|---|---|
| Flour | 1 bag | $20.00 | 20 | $1.00 | $1,000.00 |
| Sugar | 1 bag | $10.00 | 100 | $0.10 | $100.00 |
| Eggs | 1 dozen | $2.40 | 4 | $0.60 | $600.00 |
| Butter | 1 bucket | $5.00 | 10 | $0.50 | $500.00 |
| Baking Powder | 1 bag | $5.00 | 100 | $0.05 | $50.00 |
| | | | | | |
| Total Cost | | | | | $2,250.00 |

## Step 8 - Estimate cost of equipment usage (Depreciation)

| Item | I<br>Original<br>Purchase Price | J<br>Estimated life span<br>(months) | K = I/J<br>Usage Cost per month |
|---|---|---|---|
| Oven | $4,800.00 | 60 | $80.00 |
| Cake Mixer | $720.00 | 36 | $20.00 |
| Baking Pans | $180.00 | 12 | $15.00 |
| Display Shelves | $1,200.00 | 60 | $20.00 |
|  |  |  |  |
| Total Cost |  |  | $135.00 |

## Step 9 - Estimate monthly operating expenses

| Item | L<br>Cost |
|---|---|
| Sales Clerk Salary | $2,000.00 |
| Baker's wages | $1,000.00 |
| Gas and Electric | $300.00 |
| Shop Rent | $600.00 |
| Advertising | $100.00 |
|  |  |
| Total Cost | $4,000.00 |

## Step 10- Finalize budget

### SWEET ABBY BAKERY
### BUDGET FOR JANUARY 2014

| | | |
|---|---|---|
| Sales: | | $15,000.00 |
| | | |
| **Less Cost of Goods Sold:** | | |
| Flour | $1.000.00 | |
| Sugar | $100.00 | |
| Eggs | $600.00 | |
| Butter | $500.00 | |
| Baking Powder | $50.00 | |
| Oven | $80.00 | |
| Cake Mixer | $20.00 | |
| Baking Pans | $15.00 | |
| Baker's Wages | $1,000.00 | |
| Gas & Electric Bill | $300.00 | |
| | | -$3,665.00 |
| Gross Profit | | $11,335.00 |
| | | |
| **Operating Expenses:** | | |
| Display Shelves | $20.00 | |
| Sales Clerk Salary | $2,000.00 | |
| Shop Rent | $600.00 | |
| Advertising | $100.00 | |
| | | -$2,720.00 |
| Net Profit | | **$8,615.00** |

# BUILD A PROFIT AND LOSS STATEMENT

**Instructions: Gather business bank statements, invoices and sales records for a particular month and complete the following table.**

| ITEM | DETAILS | TOTAL AMOUNT |
|---|---|---|
| Sales/Income | List the value of items sold to customers during the month. Include items which customers have paid for and those that have been delivered but not paid for by the customers. | |
| Total Income (A) | | |
| Cost of Goods Sold (B) | Include the value of items bought to produce/ purchase products sold or deliver services rendered during the month. Examples - cost of flour, sugar and eggs for a baker, equipment rental fees for a construction business owner, or consultants' salaries for a consulting firm. | |
| Gross Profit (C) | A-B | |
| Business Operating Expenses (D) | List the cost (for the selected month) of items required to operate the business such as telephone, electric, gas, shop rent, staff salaries and bank charges | |
| Net Profit (E) | C-D | |

Build this each month and develop a habit of comparing monthly numbers to see what areas your business is doing well and areas that need improvement.

# BUILD A BALANCE SHEET

Instructions: Fill in the blank spaces. The information should be at the end of a specific period, (e.g., month end).

| CATEGORY | DETAILS | VALUE |
|---|---|---|
| Current Assets (A) | | |
| Cash | Calculate the value of cash you have in the bank (reconciled) and on hand. | |
| Accounts Receivable | This is the amount owed to you by customers for goods or services purchased. | |
| Inventory | Calculate the value of goods you are holding to sell to customers or materials which will be used in the production of goods for sale. | |
| Other Receivables | List all amounts owed to your business payable within one year. Examples include loans to employees. | |
| Fixed Assets (B) | Include the value of items which your business owns, and which have a life span greater than one year. Examples include: land, building, furniture, equipment. | |
| | | |
| Current Liabilities (D) | | |
| Accounts Payable | Include amounts your business owes to suppliers, which are due within one year. | |
| Other Payables | Include amounts owed to employees and other persons, which are due within one year. | |
| Long- Term Liabilities: (E) | Include balances on car notes, mortgage on office buildings and other business debts that are due after one year. | |
| Total Liabilities: (F) | D + E | |
| Owner's Equity/Net Assets (G) | C − F | |

## NOTES

I am very happy that I have been able to share some stories and hope that I have inspired you to keep doing the good things that you are doing and to find the strength to improve upon those things that are currently challenging you. I have deliberately kept this book short so that you won't be overwhelmed. I also want this to just be the beginning of our relationship, an introduction to the bigger discussions we will have as you grow your business. There will be challenging times, so I urge you to reach out to me for additional advice or anything else you may need to keep the flame burning.

You can reach me on my website: www.ourfinancialcoach.com, where I post articles to help people live their best financial lives possible, and I answer questions from readers like you. There is also a form on the site to contact me. In addition, you may send me emails to request consultations and speaking engagements for your group at tope@ourfinancialcoach.com. Now that we are on this journey together, let me know how your business is doing, what things you have been able to accomplish, and definitely what questions you have.

I wish you all the best!

# ABOUT TOPE GANIYAH FAJINGBESI

I am an international Chartered Accountant (ACA) and a Certified Public Accountant (CPA) based in Washington, D.C. I have 15 years' accounting and financial management experience working with Big Four public accounting firms, Fortune 500 corporations, and nonprofit organizations across the USA and Africa. I also hold a Bachelors degree in Accounting from the University of Lagos, Nigeria, and a Masters in Business Administration from the Goizueta Business School at Emory University in Atlanta, Georgia, USA.

In addition to my professional accounting career, I co-founded and serve as the Volunteer Executive Director of United for Kids Foundation, a tax-exempt nonprofit dedicated to providing educational and health-care opportunities to less-privileged children in Nigeria.

I developed a strong passion for personal finance at the young age of ten, when I fell in love at first sight with the "cash book" my business studies teacher had drawn up on the class blackboard. In fact, I was so enthralled that I saved my entire allowance for the whole school term, a habit my class teacher found so fascinating that he noted my thrift-iness in the Comments section of my report card. I mentioned in my acknowledgment that my parents taught me more financial manage-ment than any professor ever could. I remember how my dad made my siblings and I write, cost and justify the list of grocery items we wished to take to boarding house when we were in secondary (middle and high) school. I also recall the fact that allowances tied to responsible behavior made me think twice about my actions.

As I grew older and began to participate actively in my community and understand my Islamic faith, I realized that financial management is not only essential for personal wealth creation but also for mental and spiritual wellbeing, successful family relations and, most impor-tantly, peaceful coexistence in different societies. I was determined as a little child to create a good environment that would reduce finan-cial stress in my life. I now like to encourage little kids who exhibit enterprising behavior really early in life because they remind me of myself and my younger siblings who used to put on musical and theater performances for relatives and neighbors for token fees. All these experiences and thoughts really made it a natural decision to major in accounting in the university.

In addition to creating a much better world for children from low-income families through United for Kids Foundation, my other life mission is teaching and inspiring people, especially women, minorities and small business owners, personal finance concepts in clear and easy-to-understand language. I merge my hobbies (traveling and writing) with my deep love for my home country, Nigeria, and my Islamic faith by writing a personal finance column in Azizah magazine, visiting Nigeria regularly and blogging about personal finance at www.ourfinancialcoach.com.

I *don't want to be an instructor,*
*I want to be a teacher.*
*Teaching is my mission*
*And writing is my passion.*
*It is the skill I hold in trust.*
*I merge teaching and writing*
*To help my audience connect with my words*
*And thus find the strength to make positive changes.*
*-Tope Ganiyah Fajingbesi*

Made in the USA
Charleston, SC
19 June 2013